# LITTLE GOLDEN BOOK® CLASSICS
## A second collection featuring the art of Gustaf Tenggren

## *Three Best-Loved Tales*

### THE SHY LITTLE KITTEN
By Cathleen Schurr

❧

### THE LION'S PAW
By Jane Werner Watson

❧

### THE SAGGY BAGGY ELEPHANT
By Kathryn and Byron Jackson

The publisher wishes to thank the Kerlan Collection, University of Minnesota, for use of the original illustrations by Gustaf Tenggren.

A GOLDEN BOOK • NEW YORK
Western Publishing Company, Inc., Racine, Wisconsin 53404

# THE SHY LITTLE KITTEN

By Cathleen Schurr

Way up in the hayloft of an old red barn
lived a mother cat and her new baby kittens.
There were five bold and frisky little roly-poly
black and white kittens, and *one* little striped
kitten who was very, very shy.

One day the five bold little roly-poly black and white kittens and the one little roly-poly striped kitten who was very, very shy all sat down and washed their faces and paws with busy little red tongues.

They smoothed down their soft baby fur and
stroked their whiskers and followed their mother
down the ladder from the hayloft—jump, jump,
jump!

Then off they marched, straight out of the cool, dark barn, into the warm sunshine. How soft the grass felt under their paws! The five bold and frisky kittens rolled over in the grass and kicked up their heels with joy.

But the shy little striped kitten just stood off
by herself at the very end of the line.

That was how she happened to see the earth
push up in a little mound right in front of her.
Then—*pop!*— up came a pointed little nose. The
nose belonged to a chubby mole.

"Good morning!" said the mole, as friendly
as you please.

"Won't you come for a walk with me?"

"Oh," said the shy little kitten. She looked
shyly over her shoulder.

But the mother cat and her five bold and
frisky kittens had disappeared from sight.

So the shy little kitten went walking with the chubby mole. Soon they met a speckled frog sitting near the pond.

"My, what big eyes he has!" whispered the shy little kitten. But the frog had sharp ears, too.

He chuckled. "My mouth is much bigger. Look!" And the frog opened his great cave of a mouth.

The mole and the kitten laughed and laughed until their sides ached.

When the kitten stopped laughing and looked around, the frog had vanished. On the pond, ripples spread out in great silver circles.

"I really should be getting back to my mother and the others," said the shy little kitten, "but I don't know where to find them."

"I'll show you," said a strange voice. And out of the bushes bounded a shaggy black puppy.

"Oh, thank you," said the shy kitten. "Good-bye, mole."

So off they went together, the shy kitten and the shaggy puppy dog. The little kitten, of course, kept her eyes shyly on the ground.

But the shaggy puppy stopped to bark, "Woof, woof," at a red squirrel in a tree. He was full of mischief.

"Chee, chee, chee," the squirrel chattered
back. And she dropped a hickory nut right on
the puppy's nose. She was very brave.

"Wow, wow, wow," barked the mischievous puppy, and off they went toward the farm.

Soon they came bounding out of the woods, and there before them stretched the farmyard.

"Here we are," said the shaggy puppy dog. So down the hillside they raced, across the bridge above the brook, and straight on into the farmyard.

In the middle of the farmyard was the mother cat with her five bold and frisky little black and white kittens. In a flash the mother cat was beside her shy kitten, licking her all over with a warm red tongue.

"Where have you been?" she cried. "We're all ready to start on a picnic."

The picnic was for all the farmyard animals. There were seeds for the chickens, water bugs for the ducks, and carrots and cabbages for the rabbits. There were flies for the frogs, and there was a trough of mash for the pig.

Yum, yum, yum! How good it all was!

After they had finished eating, everyone was just beginning to feel comfortable and drowsy, when suddenly the frog jumped straight into the air, eyes almost popping out of his head.

"Help! Run!" he cried.

The frog made a leap for the brook.

Everyone scrambled after him and tumbled into the water.

"What is it?" asked the shy little kitten.

"A bee!" groaned the frog. "I bit a bee!"

Then they saw that one side of his mouth was puffed up like a green balloon.

Everybody laughed. They couldn't help it.
Even the frog laughed. They all looked so funny
as they climbed out of the brook.

The shy little kitten stood off to one side. She felt so good that she turned a backward somersault, right in the long meadow grass. "This is the best day ever," said the shy little kitten.

# THE LION'S PAW

*A Tale of African Animals*

By Jane Werner Watson

"Ow!" roared the lion.
"There is a thorn in my paw.
Who will take it out?"

"Not I," said the solid rhinoceros.
"I am whetting my pointed horn."

"Not I," said the startled kudu.
"I am racing away from here."

"Not I," the tall giraffe whispered among the tip-top leaves.

"Not I," said the bouncing baboon.
"I am having too much fun."

"Who will take the thorn out?"
cried the crowned crane flying by.

"Not I," said the hippopotamus.
"I am snuffling in the mud."

"Not I," said the small striped zebra.
"I am kicking up my heels."

"Not I," said the bright-eyed monkey.
"I am swinging by my tail."

"Not I," said the big gorilla.
"I am scratching away my fleas."

"Not I," said the elegant gazelle.
"I am leaping across the veld."

"Will no one remove the thorn?"
called the ibis over the purple pool.

"Not I," said the slippery crocodile,
smiling a hungry smile.

"Not I," said the trumpeting elephant.
"I am taking a shower bath."

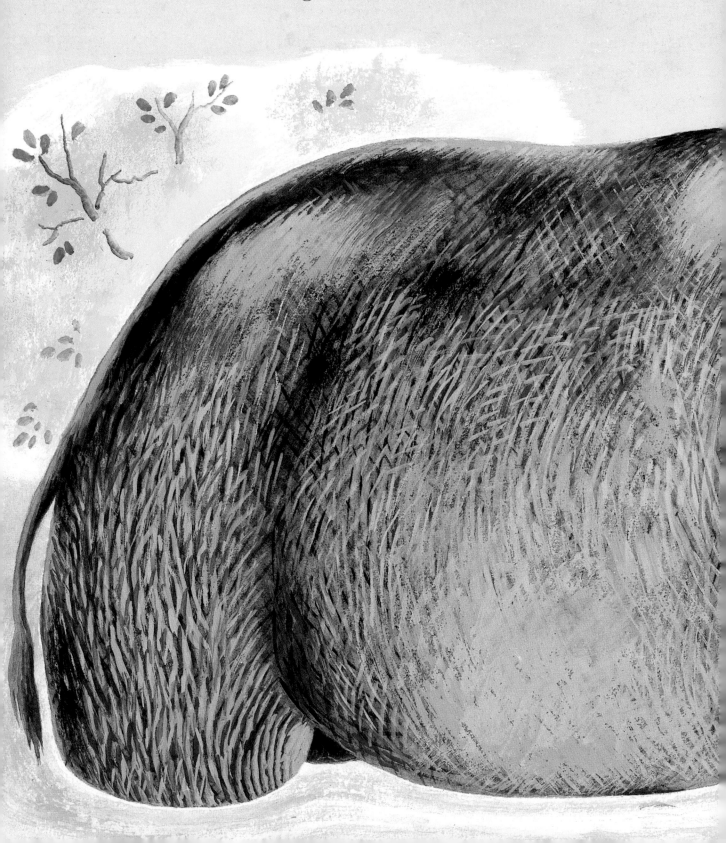

"Not I," said the leopard.
"I am slinking through the spotted shade."

"Not I," said the solemn buffalo.
"I have too much work to do."

"Who will help Lion?" cried the ostrich over the desert sands.

"Not I," said the sulky camel.
"I am chewing my chewy cud."

"Not I," said the swooping vulture.
"I'm busy hunting a meal."

"Not I," said the spotted cheetah.
"I'm busy hunting, too."

"I will, then," said the little mouse.
And do you know?
She did!

# THE SAGGY
# BAGGY ELEPHANT

By Kathryn and Byron Jackson

A happy little elephant was dancing
through the jungle. He thought he was dancing
beautifully, one-two-three-kick. But whenever he
went one-two-three, his big feet pounded so that
they shook the whole jungle. And whenever he
went kick, he kicked over a tree or a bush.

The little elephant danced along, leaving wreckage behind him, until one day he met a parrot.

"Why are you shaking the jungle all to pieces?" cried the parrot, who had never before seen an elephant. "What kind of animal are you, anyway?"

The little elephant said, "I don't know what kind of animal I am. I live all alone in the jungle. I dance and I kick—and I call myself Sooki. It's a good-sounding name, and it fits me, don't you think?"

"Maybe," answered the parrot, "but if it does it's the only thing that *does* fit you. Your ears are too big for you, and your nose is away too big for you. And your skin is *much*, MUCH too big for you. It's baggy and saggy. You should call yourself Saggy-Baggy!"

Sooki sighed. His pants *did* look pretty wrinkled.

"I'll be glad to improve myself," he said, "but I don't know how to go about it. What shall I do?"

"I can't tell you. I never saw anything like you in all my life!" replied the parrot.

The little elephant tried to smooth out his skin. He rubbed it with his trunk. That did no good.

He pulled up his pants legs—but they fell right back into dozens of wrinkles.

It was very disappointing, and the parrot's saucy laugh didn't help a bit.

Just then a tiger came walking along. He was a beautiful sleek tiger. His skin fit him like a glove.

Sooki rushed up
to him and said,
"Tiger, please tell me
why your skin fits so
well! The parrot says
mine is all baggy and
saggy, and I do want
to make it fit me like yours fits you!"

The tiger didn't care a fig about Sooki's
troubles, but he did feel flattered and important,
and he did feel just a little mite hungry.

"My skin always did fit," said the tiger. "Maybe
it's because I take a lot of exercise. But," added
the tiger, "if you don't care for exercise, I shall
be delighted to nibble a few of those extra
pounds of skin off for you!"

"Oh, no, thank you! No, thank you!" cried
Sooki. "I love exercise! Just watch me!"

Sooki ran until he was well beyond reach.

Then he did somersaults and rolled on his back. He walked on his hind legs and he walked on his front legs.

When Sooki wandered down to the river to get a big drink of water, he met the parrot. The parrot laughed harder than ever.

"I tried exercising," sighed the little elephant. "Now I don't know what to do."

"Soak in the water the way the crocodile does," laughed the parrot. "Maybe your skin will shrink."

So Sooki tramped straight into the water.

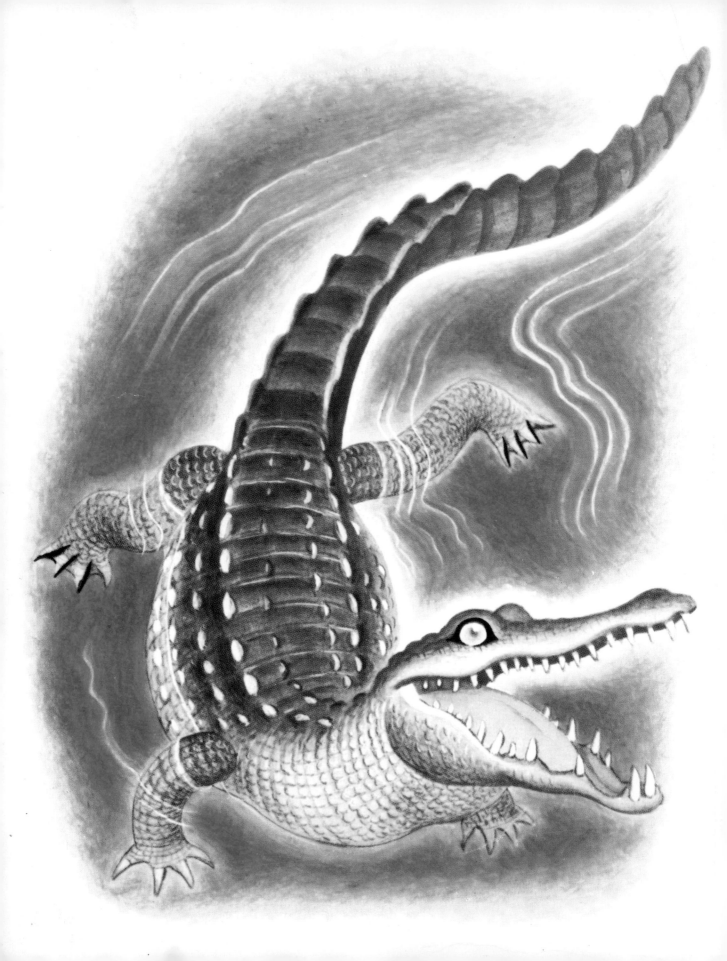

But before he had soaked nearly long enough
to shrink his skin, a great big crocodile came
swimming up, snapping his fierce jaws and
looking greedily at Sooki's tender ears.

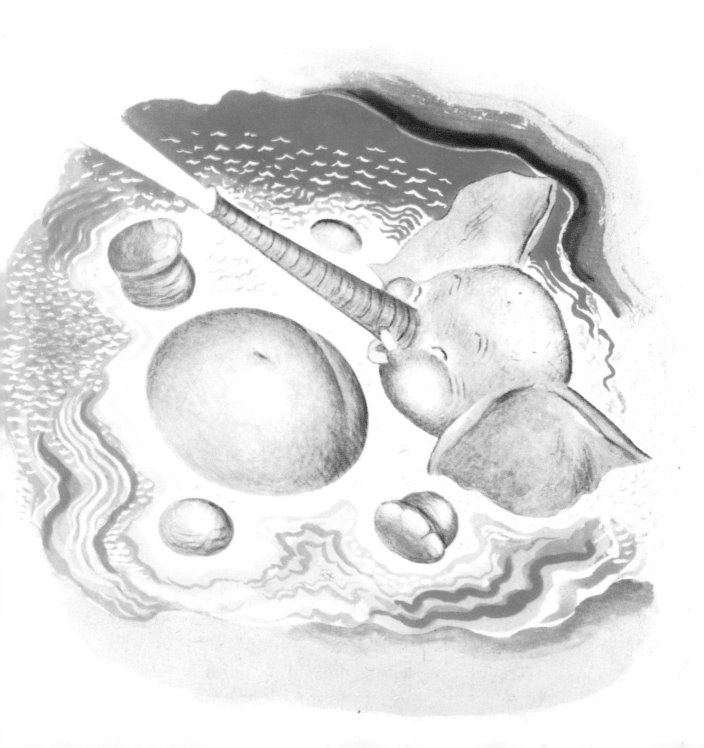

The little elephant clambered up the bank
and ran away, feeling very discouraged.

"I'd better hide in a dark place where my bags
and sags and creases and wrinkles won't show,"
he said.

By and by he found a deep dark cave, and with
a heavy sigh he tramped inside and sat down.

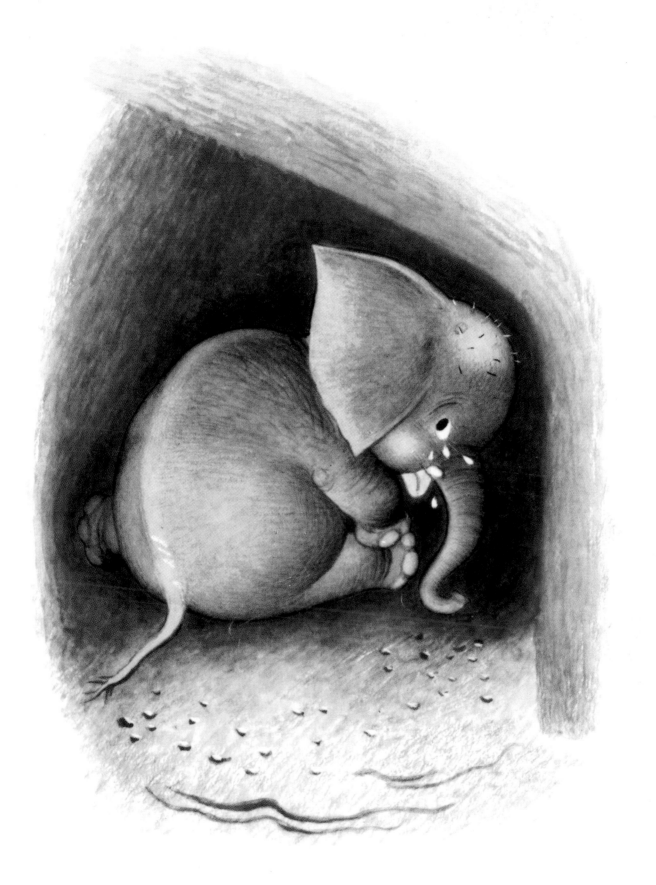

Suddenly he heard a fierce growling and grumbling and snarling. He peeped out of the cave and saw a lion padding down the path.

"I'm hungry!" roared the lion. "I haven't had a thing to eat today. Not a thing except a thin, bony antelope, and a puny monkey—and a buffalo, but such a tough one! And two turtles, but you can't count turtles. There's nothing much to eat between those saucers they wear for clothes! I'm *hungry!* I could eat an *elephant!*"

And he began to pad straight toward the dark cave where the little elephant was hidden.

"This is the end of me—sags, bags, wrinkles, and all," thought Sooki, and he let out one last, trumpeting bellow!

Just as he did, the jungle was filled with a
terrible crashing and an awful stomping. A
whole herd of great gray wrinkled elephants
came charging up, and the big hungry lion
jumped up in the air, turned around, and ran
away as fast as he could go.

Sooki peeped out of the cave and all the big
elephants smiled at him. Sooki thought they were
the most beautiful creatures he had ever seen.

"I wish I looked just like you," he said.
"You do," grinned the elephants. "You're
a perfectly dandy little elephant!"
And that made Sooki so happy that he

began to dance one-two-three-kick through the jungle, with all those big, brave, friendly elephants behind him. The saucy parrot watched them dance. But this time he didn't laugh, not even to himself.

# *About* Gustaf Tenggren

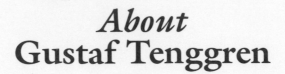

This highly talented illustrator was born in Magra, Sweden, in 1896. Both his father and grandfather were artists. Gustaf Tenggren once described the influence his grandfather especially had had on him. "Summers were happily spent in the country," he said, "tagging along with my grandfather, who was a woodcarver and painter and also a fine companion for a small boy. I never tired of watching him carve or mix the colors he used."

The young Tenggren entered art school at the age of thirteen. Before he was twenty or had yet graduated from the art school in Gothenburg, he was commissioned to illustrate his first children's book. Three years later he emigrated to the United States, settling finally in New York. "For many years," he said, "my studio was in this great city." As the years passed, he grew increasingly popular as a children's book illustrator.

In the late 1930s Gustaf Tenggren worked at the Disney Studio in California, designing both characters and backgrounds for such classic Disney films as *Snow White* and *Pinocchio*. After working with Disney, Tenggren devoted himself exclusively to children's books, including more than two dozen rich and varied titles for Golden Books.

*The Saggy Baggy Elephant,* included in this volume, is one of Tenggren's most popular Little Golden Books. The story has not been out of print since 1947, when it was first published. The innocent little elephant character is well known throughout the world. Gustaf Tenggren was also the original illustrator of *The Poky Little Puppy,* the most successful of all his Golden Books. Aside from his fanciful animal books, Tenggren also illustrated major classical works for Golden, including *Tales From the Arabian Nights, The Canterbury Tales of Geoffrey Chaucer,* and *King Arthur and the Knights of the Round Table*.

The gifted artist, who died in 1970, was once asked what children's book illustration meant to him. "I find this work very rewarding," he answered, "as it seems to give so much pleasure to so many children."